CHEVROLET
8
19

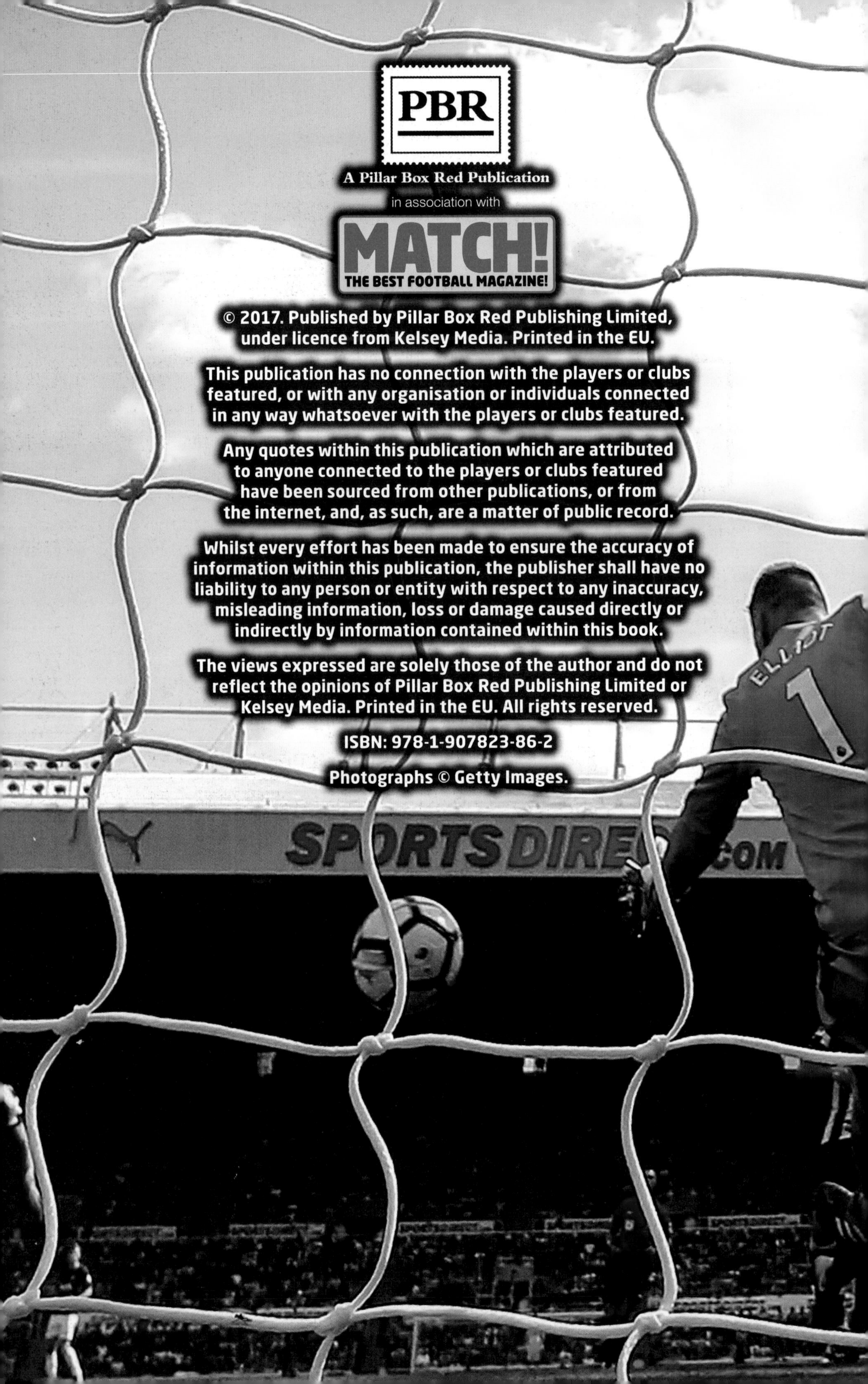

PBR

A Pillar Box Red Publication

in association with

MATCH!

THE BEST FOOTBALL MAGAZINE!

This publication has no connection with the players or clubs featured, or with any organisation or individuals connected in any way whatsoever with the players or clubs featured.

Any quotes within this publication which are attributed to anyone connected to the players or clubs featured have been sourced from other publications, or from the internet, and, as such, are a matter of public record.

Whilst every effort has been made to ensure the accuracy of information within this publication, the publisher shall have no liability to any person or entity with respect to any inaccuracy, misleading information, loss or damage caused directly or indirectly by information contained within this book.

ISBN: 978-1-907823-86-2

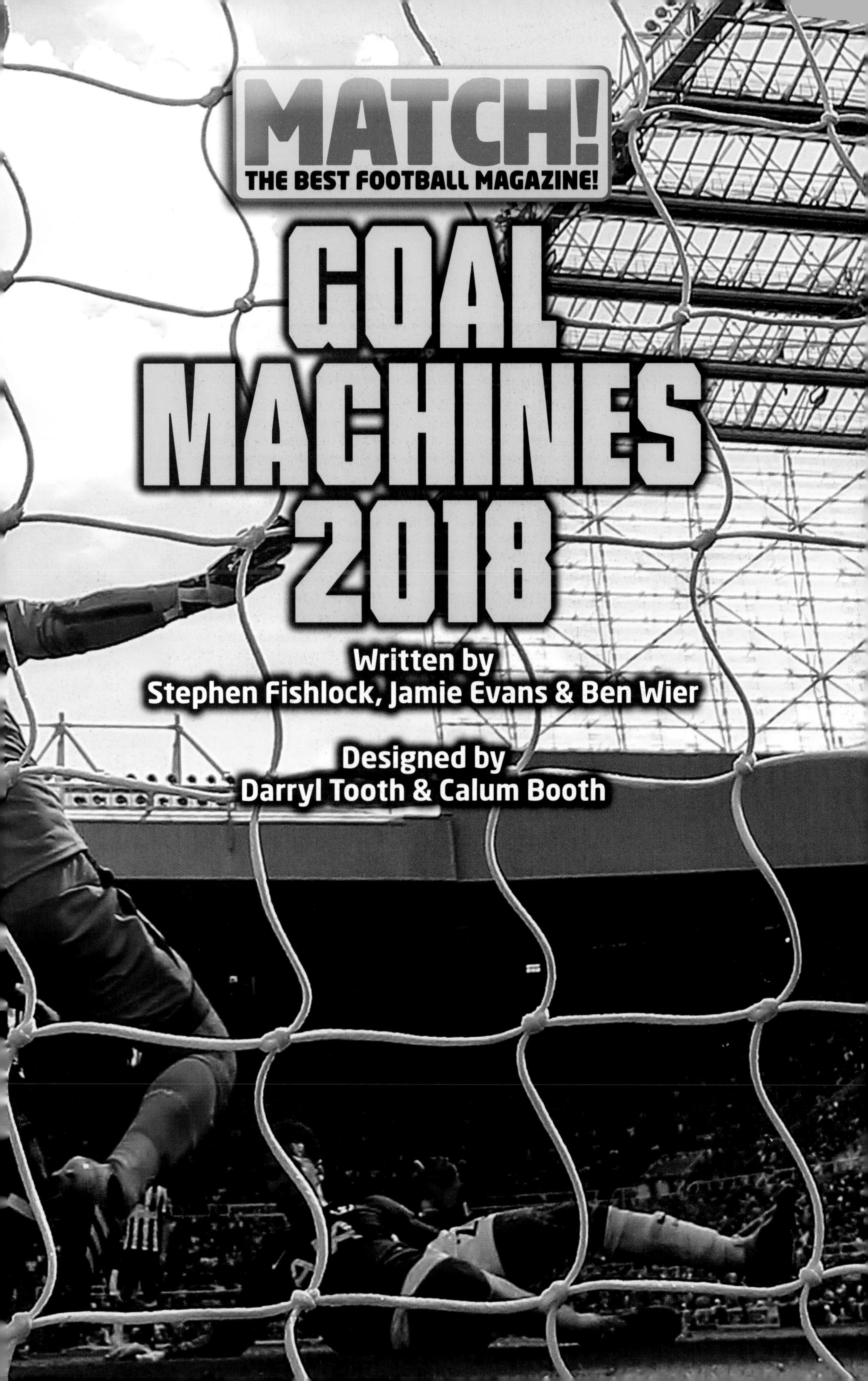

MATCH!
THE BEST FOOTBALL MAGAZINE!

GOAL MACHINES 2018

Written by
Stephen Fishlock, Jamie Evans & Ben Wier

Designed by
Darryl Tooth & Calum Booth

CONTENTS

STAT ATTACK!
PREMIER LEAGUE GOAL MACHINES
260
0.68
11
183
31
1
7
5
11
4

Troy Deeney
Arkadiusz Milik
Nikola Kalinic
Samuel Eto'o
Didier Drogba
Marcus Rashford

STAT ATTACK!
LA LIGA GOAL MACHINES
349
35
7
4
6
19
32
27
82
4

QUIZ 1
GOAL MACHINES BRAIN-BUSTER
FACE IN THE CROWD
ACE QUIZZES 28 & 48

STAT ATTACK!
REST OF EUROPE GOAL MACHINES
EUROPE STAT ATTACK 34

DRAW YOUR FAVE GOAL MACHINE!
You've seen our countdown of the Top 100 Goal Machines – now why not sketch your fave star for the chance to win an ace prize?
WIN!
DRAW YOUR FAVE GOAL MACHINE 58

Bertrand Traore

100

Club: *Lyon* **DOB:** *6/9/95*

Country: *Burkina Faso*

The new Lyon star can play on the wing or up front, and tests opponents with his rapid pace and power! His goals helped fire Ajax to the Europa League final in 2016-17, and MATCH reckons the versatile youngster has a massive future ahead of him!

Aleksandar Mitrovic

99

Club: *Newcastle* **DOB:** *16/9/94*

Country: *Serbia*

Mitrovic earned his move to England by scoring 44 goals in 90 games for Anderlecht, and ripping it up for Serbia's U21s! He hasn't quite set the world alight for Newcastle yet, but we think it's only a matter of time before the Magpies man does!

Ruben Castro

98

Club: *Guizhou Zhicheng*

Country: *Spain* **DOB:** *27/6/81*

Ace hitman Castro is currently on loan in China after banging in the goals in Spain for over a decade! In seven seasons at Real Betis, the net-buster fired the club to promotion on two separate occasions, and became their all-time top scorer in 2014-15!

Islam Slimani

97

Club: *Leicester* **DOB:** *18/6/88*

Country: *Algeria*

Leicester's record signing had a slow start to life in England, but still hit eight goals in his debut season – including a Champions League winner against Porto. At Sporting, he scored 27 league goals in 2015-16, plus he has a quality international record too!

Fernando Torres

96

Club: *Atletico Madrid*
Country: *Spain* **DOB:** *20/3/84*

Antoine Griezmann is the main man at Atletico, but ex-Prem ace Torres still offers plenty! As he's got older, El Nino has changed his style of play to become a real workhorse striker, but he still scores the odd goal – 22 in his last two seasons in fact!

Tiquinho Soares

95

Club: *Porto* **DOB:** *17/1/91*
Country: *Brazil*

Portugal's developed some class South American talent recently, and Tiquinho could be the next big thing! Porto snapped him up after he scored seven goals in 16 games for Vitoria, and he carried on that form for Porto – netting 12 in his first 15 matches. Hero!

Wayne Rooney

94

Club: *Everton* **DOB:** *24/10/85*
Country: *England*

As the all-time top scorer for both England and Man. United, there's no doubt Rooney is a goalscoring legend! Although he's past his best now, at his peak he was capable of scoring any type of goal, and he's still got some magic left in his boots!

Heung-Min Son

93

Club: *Tottenham* **DOB:** *8/7/92*

Country: *South Korea*

The Spurs speed demon's darting runs, ability to shrug off FBs and ice-cool finishing bagged him a place in our Top 100 list! He's an unstoppable force when he's on his game – which he showed by ripping net 21 times in all comps last season. What a legend!

Iago Aspas

92

Club: *Celta Vigo* **DOB:** *1/8/87*

Country: *Spain*

After a disastrous spell with Liverpool, Aspas returned to his boyhood club in 2015 with a point to prove – and boy did he succeed! In 2016-17, nobody outside of Barça or Real Madrid scored more La Liga goals than the Celta star's 19. He's deadly!

Philippe Coutinho

91

Club: *Liverpool* **DOB:** *12/6/92*

Country: *Brazil*

Nobody scored more goals for Liverpool in 2016-17, and most of them were absolute belters! The Samba star has always had screamers in his locker, but after learning to time his runs into the box better too, he's turning into a proper goal machine!

Lorenzo Insigne

90

Club: *Napoli* **DOB:** *4/6/91*

Country: *Italy*

Napoli have one of the best attacks in Europe, and Insigne plays a massive part in that! The wicked winger is a tricky dribbler who loves beating defenders and getting into the box, and with 30 Serie A goals in two seasons, he's lethal when given a chance!

Chris Wood

89

Club: *Burnley* **DOB:** *7/12/91*

Country: *New Zealand*

New Zealand hitman Wood had been a solid Championship striker for a few years, but finally delivered on his big potential with 27 goals in 2016-17. After a club-record £15 million move to Burnley, now he wants to prove he can cut it in the Prem!

Tammy Abraham

88

Club: *Swansea* **DOB:** *2/10/97*

Country: *England*

Tammy had a quality record at youth level for Chelsea - hitting 74 goals in 98 matches - and he took that form straight into the Championship. The wonderkid scored 26 times on loan at Bristol City, and will definitely be one to watch at Swansea in 2017-18!

Tim Cahill

87

Club: *Melbourne City*

Country: *Australia* **DOB:** *6/12/79*

Even though he's nearing his 40s, Cahill is still banging the goals in! The ace Aussie had a quality Prem career with Everton, where his timing, movement and heading made him a huge threat! It's no surprise the attacker is his country's record goalscorer!

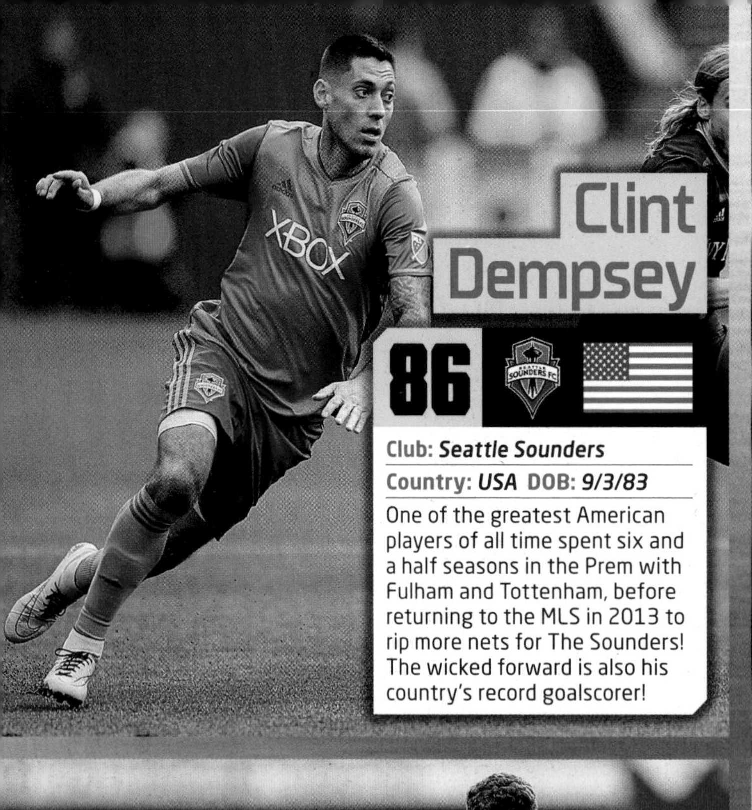

Clint Dempsey

86

Club: *Seattle Sounders*

Country: *USA* **DOB:** *9/3/83*

One of the greatest American players of all time spent six and a half seasons in the Prem with Fulham and Tottenham, before returning to the MLS in 2013 to rip more nets for The Sounders! The wicked forward is also his country's record goalscorer!

Dwight Gayle

85

Club: *Newcastle* **DOB:** *17/10/90*

Country: *England*

After being released by Arsenal as a youngster, Gayle had to battle his way back to the top through non-league football. Newcastle fans will be glad he never gave up - his 23 goals in 2016-17 helped fire The Magpies back to the Premier League!

Andre Gray

84

Club: *Watford* **DOB:** *26/6/91*

Country: *England*

Gray worked his way up from non-league like Gayle too, and was prolific for Hinckley, Luton and Brentford before Burnley made him their record signing in 2015. Watford will want more goals from the speedster after spending £18.5 million on him!

Joshua King

83

Club: *Bournemouth*

Country: *Norway* **DOB:** *15/1/92*

Under Eddie Howe, King has finally started to deliver on the promise he showed as a young gun at Man. United. The Norway ace ended 2016-17 with 16 Prem goals - including 12 in his last 16 matches! His electric pace makes him a threat to anyone!

Peter Crouch

82

Club: *Stoke* **DOB:** *30/1/81*

Country: *England*

Nobody has scored more Prem headers than Crouchy, but the target man has loads more to his game than just aerial ability - he is unselfish and helps link up Stoke's attacking play! The 6ft 7in striker hit 22 goals in 42 games for England, too!

Sandro Ramirez

81

Club: *Everton* **DOB:** *9/7/95*

Country: *Spain*

The Barça academy graduate has always had bags of potential, and finally delivered on it for Malaga in 2016-17. Sandro scored 14 La Liga goals for the Spanish side to earn a £5.2 million move to Everton, and the young striker could prove to be a real bargain!

STAT ATTACK!

PREMIER LEAGUE GOAL MACHINES

260

The Premier League's all-time top scorer is Alan Shearer – he bagged 260 goals combined for Blackburn and Newcastle!

0.68

Arsenal legend Thierry Henry's goals-to-game ratio of 0.68 is the best strike rate of any player in the Prem's top ten scorers!

11

Leicester hitman Jamie Vardy scored in an epic 11 consecutive games during The Foxes' title-winning season of 2015-16!

183

Wayne Rooney holds the Premier League record for most goals at a single club – 183 for Man. United – and most away goals – 90!

176

Sadio Mane has hit the quickest Prem hat-trick – it took him just 176 seconds to bag a treble for Southampton against Aston Villa in May 2015!

31

Cristiano Ronaldo, Alan Shearer and Luis Suarez hold the record for most goals in a 38-game Premier League season!

1

In 2016-17, Tottenham's Harry Kane became the first Englishman to win consecutive Prem Golden Boots since Michael Owen in 1997-98 and 1998-99!

7

Craig Bellamy is the only player to score for seven different Prem teams – Coventry, Newcastle, Blackburn, Liverpool, West Ham, Man. City and Cardiff!

5

Only five players have scored five goals in a single Prem game – Sergio Aguero, Dimitar Berbatov, Jermain Defoe, Alan Shearer and Andy Cole!

11

The record for most hat-tricks scored in Prem history belongs to Alan Shearer – he hit 11, two more than Liverpool legend Robbie Fowler!

4

Thierry Henry won four Prem Golden Boots for Arsenal between 2002 and 2006 – more than any player in Premier League history. Ledge!

Troy Deeney

80

Club: *Watford* **DOB:** *29/6/88*

Country: *England*

Nobody's played a bigger role than Deeney in Watford's rise to the Prem! Troy hit 21 goals as The Hornets were promoted from the Championship in 2015, and he's netted double figures in both of his top-flight seasons too, taking him to 100 league goals!

Arkadiusz Milik

79

Club: *Napoli* **DOB:** *28/2/94*

Country: *Poland*

A bad knee injury ruined Milik's first season at Napoli after he joined the Serie A giants for £29.6 million in 2016. The ace striker is a class finisher when fit though, and caught Europe's attention by smashing 47 goals in two seasons for Ajax. Lethal!

Samuel Eto'o

78

Club: *Antalyaspor* **DOB:** *10/3/81*

Country: *Cameroon*

At his peak, Eto'o was one of the best goalscorers in the world! He netted in Barça's 2006 and 2009 CL wins, and played a huge role in lifting the trophy for Inter in 2010 too. The Cameroon ledge is still going strong in Turkey – ripping it up for Antalyaspor!

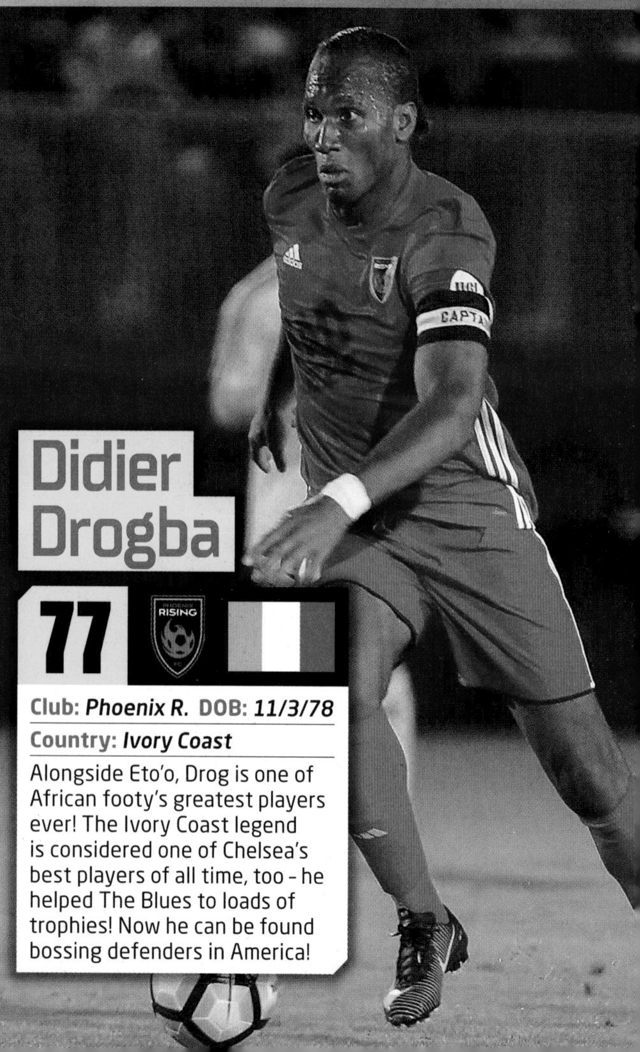

Didier Drogba

77

Club: *Phoenix R.* **DOB:** *11/3/78*

Country: *Ivory Coast*

Alongside Eto'o, Drog is one of African footy's greatest players ever! The Ivory Coast legend is considered one of Chelsea's best players of all time, too – he helped The Blues to loads of trophies! Now he can be found bossing defenders in America!

Nikola Kalinic

76

Club: *AC Milan* **DOB:** *5/1/88*

Country: *Croatia*

Prem fans might remember Kalinic's unsuccessful spell at Blackburn, but since leaving England the Croatia striker has been banging in the goals for Dnipro and Fiorentina! Now he's on loan at AC Milan, he's ready to continue owning Serie A!

Marcus Rashford

75

Club: *Man. United* **DOB:** *31/10/97*

Country: *England*

All eyes are on Old Trafford this season to see if Rash can fulfil his massive potential! His first full season at United didn't quite hit top gear, but there was defo glimpses of his talent. We think double figures for Prem goals will be a good campaign for him!

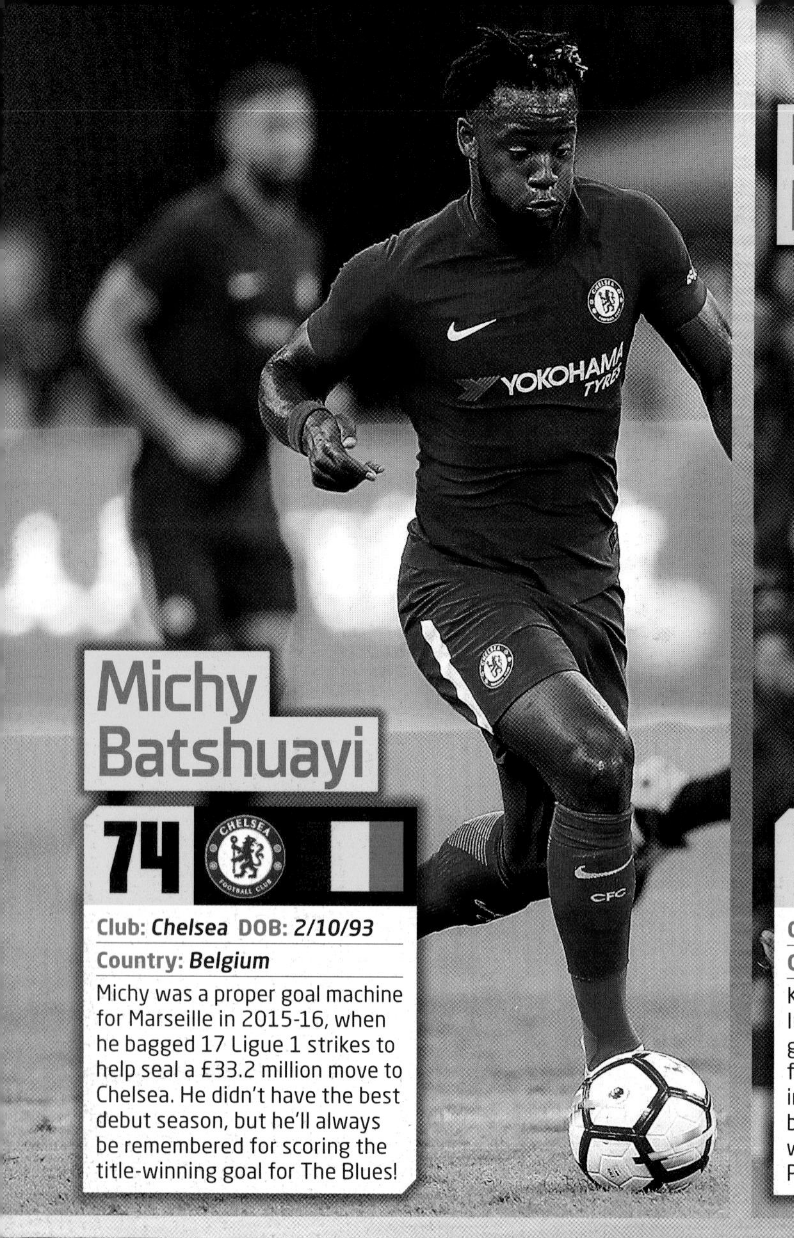

Michy Batshuayi

74

Club: *Chelsea* **DOB:** *2/10/93*
Country: *Belgium*

Michy was a proper goal machine for Marseille in 2015-16, when he bagged 17 Ligue 1 strikes to help seal a £33.2 million move to Chelsea. He didn't have the best debut season, but he'll always be remembered for scoring the title-winning goal for The Blues!

Robbie Keane

73

Club: *Atl. Kolkata* **DOB:** *8/7/80*
Country: *Republic Of Ireland*

Keane's record of 68 goals for Ireland makes him their highest goalscorer of all time, and only four Europeans have more at international level! The penalty-box predator knows exactly where the net is – 126 career Prem goals proves just that!

Nicolai Jorgensen

72

Club: *Feyenoord* **DOB:** *15/1/91*
Country: *Denmark*

Jorgensen followed in the footsteps of legends like Luis Suarez and Ruud van Nistelrooy by winning the Eredivisie Golden Boot in 2016-17, as he smashed 21 goals to help the club to their first league title in 18 years! He's a proper powerhouse hitman!

Luuk de Jong

71

Club: *PSV* **DOB:** *27/8/90*

Country: *Holland*

De Jong has been a quality goal scorer for PSV since returning to the Eredivisie in 2014, averaging better than a goal every other game! He's a proper No.9 who dominates in the air - around half of his strikes for the Dutch giants have been with his head!

Manolo Gabbiadini

70

Club: *Southampton*

Country: *Italy* **DOB:** *26/11/91*

The Southampton star's left foot is one of the most lethal in the Premier League! He's proved to be a quality signing for The Saints since joining from Napoli in January 2017, and a top season for them will see him go to the World Cup with Italy. Legend!

Anthony Martial

69

Club: *Man. United* **DOB:** *5/12/95*

Country: *France*

Martial's pace convinced United to make him the most expensive teenager ever when they signed him from Monaco in 2015! His sick debut goal against Liverpool made him an immediate hero to the Old Trafford fans, but they want to see more from him!

Gylfi Sigurdsson

68

Club: *Everton* **DOB:** *8/9/89*

Country: *Iceland*

Swansea would have definitely been relegated without Gylfi's goals and assists in 2016-17! The playmaker's ability to strike the ball with deadly accuracy makes him a threat from anywhere, and that's why Everton splashed out a massive £45 million on him!

STAT ATTACK!

LA LIGA GOAL MACHINES

35

Real Madrid legend Raul and Lionel Messi hold the joint-record for most La Liga teams scored against – 35!

7

Barcelona legend Laszlo Kubala and Athletic Bilbao hero Bata are the only players ever to score seven goals in a single La Liga game!

19

onaldo, Lionel Messi and Cristiano Ronaldo have all scored against 19 teams in a single Spanish season – a top-flight record!

32

Cristiano Ronaldo has scored the most hat-tricks in La Liga history, and also netted eight in a single season in 2014-15 to equal the league record!

82

Real Oviedo legend Isidro Langara took just 82 games to score 100 league goals, and hit three hat-tricks in a row in 1935 – both are La Liga records!

21

During the 2012-13 season, Lionel Messi scored in 21 matches on the bounce – including 33 goals in total – to set a new Spanish top-flight record. Total legend!

349

Lionel Messi is La Liga's all-time top scorer – by the end of the 2016-17 season, he'd netted 349 times for Barcelona!

4

Two players have won the Pichichi Trophy four seasons in a row – Real Madrid heroes Alfredo Di Stefano and Hugo Sanchez!

6

Telmo Zarra won La Liga's top scorer award six times for Athletic Bilbao between 1945 and 1953 – more than any player in history!

27

Cristiano Ronaldo and Leo Messi hold the record for most games scored in during a season – CR7 scored in 27 games in 2011-12, and Leo matched the feat in 2012-13!

4

Luis Suarez scored four goals in a game twice in consecutive matches for Barcelona in the 2015-16 season – he's the only player ever to do that!

Roberto Firmino

67

Club: *Liverpool* **DOB:** *2/10/91*

Country: *Brazil*

Firmino played as a DM as a kid, but you'll know him now as Liverpool's main man up front! The Samba star's work-rate and movement make him a proper nightmare to defend against, and his finishing is better than most real out-and-out strikers!

Eden Hazard

65

Club: *Chelsea* **DOB:** *7/1/91*

Country: *Belgium*

Hazard is a world-class winger with bags of skill and tons of pace, and that lethal combination allows him to get into great goal scoring positions! After a career best tally of 16 Prem goals last season, he needs to go one step better and score 20+ this year!

Klaas-Jan Huntelaar

66

Club: *Ajax* **DOB:** *12/8/83*

Country: *Holland*

Huntelaar returned to the club where he made his name as a monster No.9 in the summer of 2017, after a career at Euro giants Real Madrid, AC Milan and Schalke. He bagged 102 goals in 134 games in his first spell, and is even better this time around!

Sadio Mane

64

Club: *Liverpool* **DOB:** *10/4/92*

Country: *Senegal*

Alongside Philippe Coutinho, Mane was Liverpool's joint-top scorer in the league with 13 in 2016-17, and there's plenty more to come! He terrifies defenders with his direct running, and the net rips nine times out of ten when he lets fly at goal!

Pedro

63

Club: *Chelsea* **DOB:** *28/7/87*

Country: *Spain*

The La Masia academy graduate hasn't just scored loads of goals – he's scored super important ones too! He bagged in the semis and the final of Barcelona's 2011 CL victory, and scored in Chelsea's crucial win over Tottenham in their title-winning season!

Bafetimbi Gomis

62

Club: *Galatasaray* **DOB:** *6/8/85*

Country: *France*

After joining Marseille on loan from Swansea, Gomis was one of the top scorers in Ligue 1 in 2016-17, smashing 20 goals in total! His red-hot form persuaded Turkish side Galatasaray to snap him up, and the France beast looks set to rock the Super Lig!

Robin van Persie

61

Club: *Fenerbahce* DOB: *6/8/83*

Country: *Holland*

RVP was a Premier League star for years, bagging 144 goals for Arsenal and then Man. United. His move from The Gunners to Old Trafford sealed the 2012-13 title, and since leaving United his lethal left foot has continued to lash in goals at Fenerbahce!

Sebastian Giovinco

60

Club: *Toronto* DOB: *26/1/87*

Country: *Italy*

Giovinco's move to Toronto will go down as one of the best deals in MLS history! The Italian has absolutely destroyed the league, smashing in long-range screamers and topping the club's goal and assist charts every year since joining the Canadian club!

Mario Gomez

59

Club: *Wolfsburg* DOB: *10/7/85*

Country: *Germany*

Gomez has been one of the best goalscorers German football has seen in the last ten years. The super strong striker is a beast in the air, loves getting on the end of crosses, and his predatory instincts have taken him to over 150 Bundesliga goals. Wowzers!

Seydou Doumbia

58

Club: *Sporting* **DOB:** *31/12/87*
Country: *Ivory Coast*

Doumbia's scored bucketloads of goals since arriving in European footy in 2008, bagging 100+ for Young Boys and CSKA Moscow! He rediscovered his goalscoring boots at Basel last season with 20 goals in 25 games, and will get even more at Sporting!

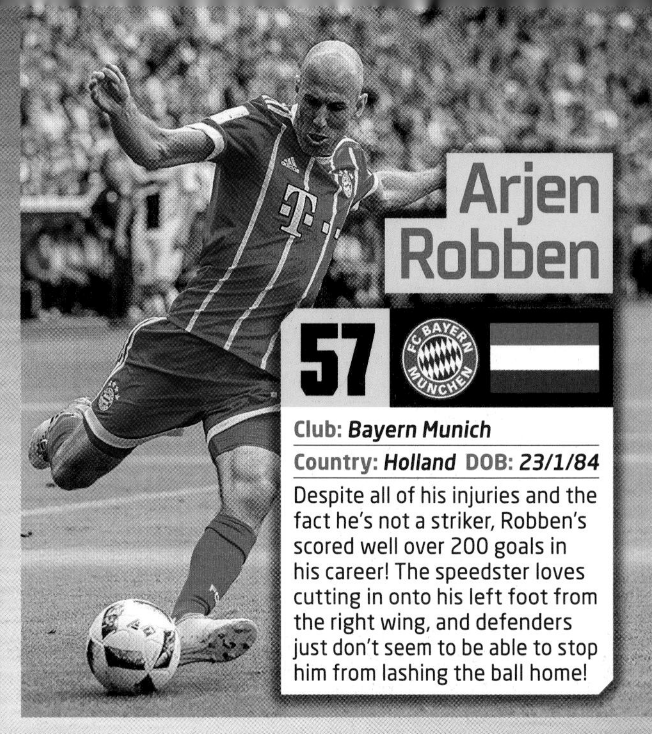

Arjen Robben

57

Club: *Bayern Munich*
Country: *Holland* **DOB:** *23/1/84*

Despite all of his injuries and the fact he's not a striker, Robben's scored well over 200 goals in his career! The speedster loves cutting in onto his left foot from the right wing, and defenders just don't seem to be able to stop him from lashing the ball home!

Kostas Mitroglou

56

Club: *Marseille* **DOB:** *12/3/88*
Country: *Greece*

Mitroglou was a total flop in the Prem, but after joining Benfica in 2016 he rediscovered the ace form that convinced Fulham to pay £12 million for him in 2014! After two seasons of ripping it up in Portugal, Kostas joined French giants Marseille last summer!

Leigh Griffiths

54

Club: *Celtic* **DOB:** *20/8/90*
Country: *Scotland*

Griffiths was a real goal king in the Scottish Prem while on loan at Hibernian from Wolves, and since joining Celtic in 2014, he hasn't stopped scoring! He's hit tons for The Hoops, and became a Scotland hero with two epic WC qualifying goals against England!

Fernando Llorente

55

Club: *Tottenham* **DOB:** *26/2/85*
Country: *Spain*

Spurs ace Llorente was prolific in La Liga and Serie A before joining the Prem in 2016, and his goals were crucial in keeping Swansea up last season! The target man is lethal when the ball's in the air – nobody scored more Premier League headers in 2016-17!

Cedric Bakambu

53

Club: *Villarreal* **DOB:** *11/4/91*
Country: *DR Congo*

The fast and powerful striker was the main man in Villarreal's epic Europa League campaign in 2015-16, smashing nine goals on their way to the semis! Since joining the club, Bakambu has fired The Yellow Submarine to two top-five finishes in a row!

Carlos Tevez

52

Club: *Shanghai Shenhua*
Country: *Argentina* **DOB:** *5/2/84*

Tevez has scored tons of goals in Argentina, Brazil, England and Italy throughout his ace career! He's got tons of ability and lethal finishing skills, plus the work-rate to match. The No.32 has played a key role in league title wins for Man. United, Man. City and Juve!

David Villa

51

Club: *New York City*
Country: *Spain* **DOB:** *3/12/81*

Spain's all-time top goalscorer was a La Liga ledge for Valencia, Barcelona and Atletico Madrid, and he hasn't slowed down since moving to the MLS! The ice-cool finisher's been NYC's top scorer every year, and proven he's still got razor-sharp shooting skills!

Bradley Wright-Phillips

50

Club: *NY Red Bulls*
Country: *England* **DOB:** *12/3/85*

Moving Stateside was defo the best decision Wright-Phillips ever made! After a decent EFL career at Southampton, Plymouth and Charlton, the son of Ian Wright made the move to America, and has bossed the league ever since! He's closing in on 100 MLS goals!

Mario Balotelli

49

Club: *Nice* DOB: *12/8/90*

Country: *Italy*

One of the biggest personalities in football has finally found his home! Balotelli's time with Inter, Man. City, AC Milan and Liverpool was packed with epic goals and controversial moments, but he's been class in Ligue 1, firing Nice to a top-three finish in 2016-17!

Mario Mandzukic

48

Club: *Juventus* DOB: *21/5/86*

Country: *Croatia*

We don't think Mandzukic gets the credit he deserves – he's been quality in Serie A, La Liga and the Bundesliga! One thing he does get credit for though, is scoring one of the best CL goals ever – we'll never get bored of watching his bicycle-kick against Real!

Carlos Bacca

47

Club: *Villarreal* DOB: *8/9/86*

Country: *Colombia*

Bacca was the main man in two of Sevilla's recent Europa League triumphs, firing them to glory in 2014 and 2015! The class Colombian took that form into Serie A with AC Milan, and now he's back in La Liga again with Spanish high-flyers Villarreal!

GOAL MACHINES BRAIN-BUSTER

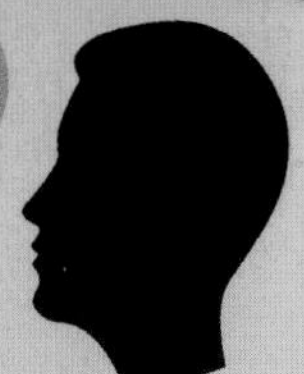

How well do you know some of footy's best goalscorers?

1. In what year did Man. City sign Argentina hitman Sergio Aguero - 2011, 2012 or 2013?

2. True or False? Lionel Messi is older than Cristiano Ronaldo!

3. What shirt number does Harry Kane wear for Spurs - No.9, No.10 or No.11?

4. Wayne Rooney has scored for two Premier League clubs - Everton and which other team?

5. What quality boot brand does Daniel Sturridge wear - Nike, adidas, New Balance or Puma?

6. Monaco striker Radamel Falcao plays international footy for which South American country?

7. Arsenal signed Chile goal machine Alexis Sanchez from which La Liga club in 2014?

8. Who was Chelsea's top scorer in the 2016-17 season?

9. Is Juventus wonderkid Paulo Dybala left or right footed?

10. What club did Poland goal king Robert Lewandowski make his Bundesliga debut for?

1 ....
2 ....
3 ....
4 ....
5 ....
6 ....
7 ....
8 ....
9 ....
10 ....

FACE IN THE CROWD

Can you spot ten legendary finishers in this pic? The stars below are all there somewhere!

Alan Shearer

Ronaldo

Ruud van Nistelrooy

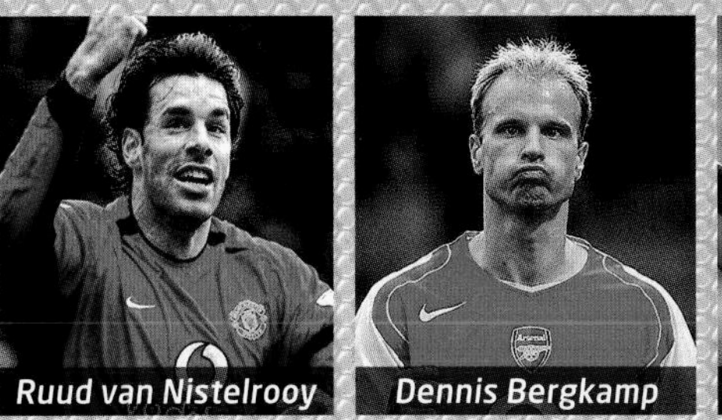
Dennis Bergkamp

Andriy Shevchenko

Michael Owen

Hernan Crespo

Henrik Larsson

Ole Gunnar Solskjaer

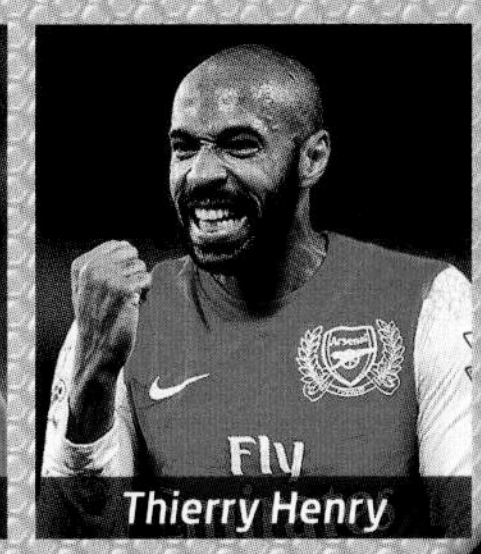
Thierry Henry

ANSWER ON PAGE

Daniel Sturridge

46

Club: *Liverpool* **DOB:** *1/9/89*

Country: *England*

Injuries have hampered Studger big-time, but he's still produced some real moments of magic in his career! He played a massive role in Liverpool's 2013-14 title bid with 21 goals, and who can forget his strike against Wales at Euro 2016? He's class on his day!

Kasper Dolberg

45

Club: *Ajax* **DOB:** *6/10/97*

Country: *Denmark*

Even though he was a teenager, Dolberg established himself as Ajax's main man in 2016-17! In his first season with the Dutch giants, he bagged a sensational 18-minute hat-trick and scored six times in total on their way to the Europa League final!

Kevin Gameiro

44

Club: *Atletico Madrid*

Country: *France* **DOB:** *9/5/87*

Gameiro was Sevilla's top scorer in their fifth Europa League win in 2016, and his eye for goal and movement make him the perfect partner at Atletico for Antoine Griezmann. The pair have been a deadly duo, combining to score 28 La Liga goals in 2016-17!

Jamie Vardy

43

Club: *Leicester* **DOB:** *11/1/87*

Country: *England*

Vardy completed a meteoric rise from non-league footy to Prem champion in 2016, smashing 24 goals in Leicester's historic title win! Not many players can match his pace and energy, and the Sheffield lad loves to smash it home when he gets a chance!

Gabriel Jesus

42

Club: *Man. City* **DOB:** *3/4/97*

Country: *Brazil*

Man. City paid £27 million to sign Gabriel from Palmeiras in 2016, and it's easy to see why! Jesus exploded onto the scene with seven goals in his first ten Prem games, plus five in his first seven for Brazil! He's definitely got the potential to win the Ballon d'Or!

Moussa Dembele

41

Club: *Celtic* **DOB:** *12/7/96*

Country: *France*

Dembele's pace and power has tied Scottish defences in knots since joining Celtic from Fulham in 2016! Alongside his 17 league goals last season, he bagged five in the Champions League – including two world-class finishes against Man. City!

Christian Benteke

40

Club: *Crystal Palace*

Country: *Belgium* **DOB:** *3/12/90*

Nobody dominates in the air like Benteke does! Since he moved to the Prem in 2012, over a third of the big Belgian's goals have come with his head, and he's almost single-handedly helped Aston Villa and Crystal Palace avoid relegation. What a beast!

Anthony Modeste

39

Club: *Tianjin Quanjian*

Country: *France* **DOB:** *14/4/88*

Modeste's been one of the most consistent scorers in Germany over the past couple of seasons, and smashed 25 goals as Cologne finished fifth in 2016-17! That attracted Chinese club Tianjin, who will pay £32 million at the end of a two-year loan spell!

Olivier Giroud

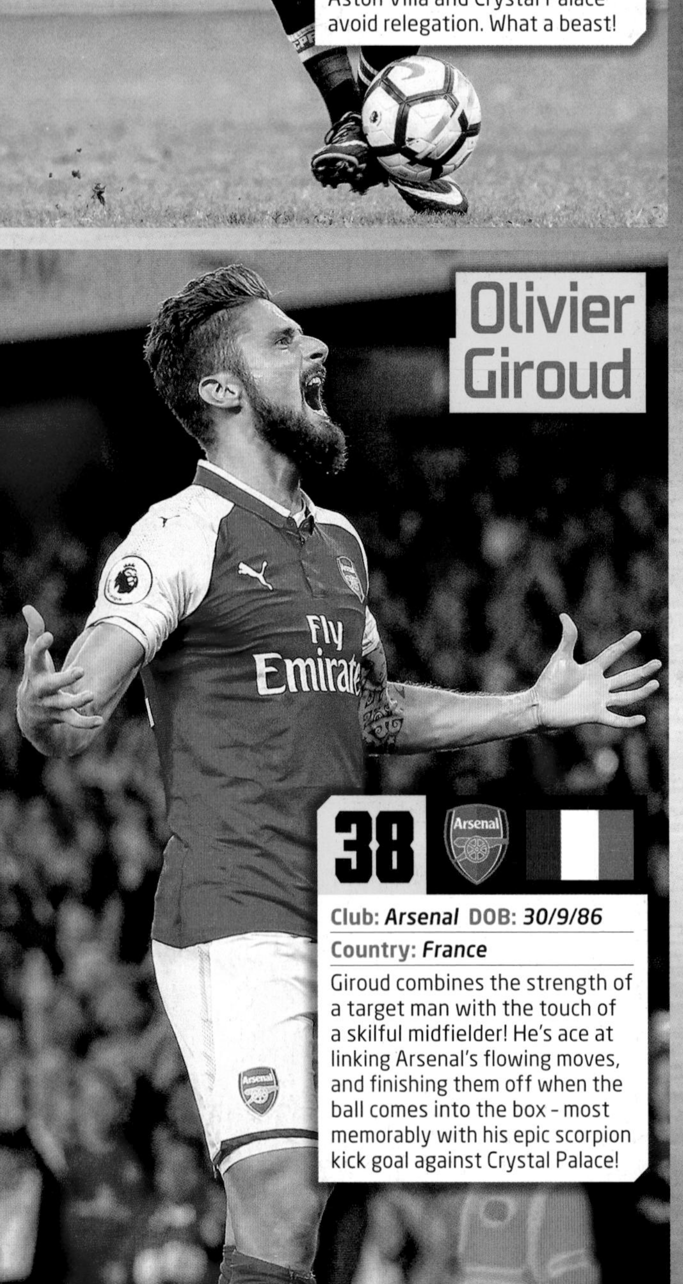

38

Club: *Arsenal* **DOB:** *30/9/86*

Country: *France*

Giroud combines the strength of a target man with the touch of a skilful midfielder! He's ace at linking Arsenal's flowing moves, and finishing them off when the ball comes into the box - most memorably with his epic scorpion kick goal against Crystal Palace!

Andre Silva

37

Club: *AC Milan* **DOB:** *6/11/95*

Country: *Portugal*

When AC Milan went looking for a goalscorer in their big summer of spending, they found the perfect man in Andre Silva! The young star has been banging them in for Porto, and has been tipped as Cristiano Ronaldo's Portugal replacement by the man himself!

Ciro Immobile

36

Club: ***Lazio*** **DOB:** ***20/2/90***

Country: ***Italy***

Immobile won the Serie A Golden Boot with Torino in 2013-14, but after tough spells at Dortmund and Sevilla, returned to Italy and hit his best form in 2016-17! His ice-cool finishing skills saw him net 23 goals for Lazio and get his place back in the Italy squad!

Timo Werner

35

Club: ***RB Leipzig*** **DOB:** ***6/3/96***

Country: ***Germany***

Bundesliga fans have known all about Werner since he made his debut as a 17-year-old, but last season was his big breakthrough! No player under 21 ripped more nets in Europe's top five leagues, and then the hitman bagged the Confederations Cup Golden Boot!

Kylian Mbappe

34  

Club: ***PSG*** **DOB:** ***20/12/98***

Country: ***France***

The hottest wonderkid on the planet spent the 2016-17 season destroying defences for Monaco in Ligue 1 and the CL with his frightening pace and dribbling! We think Mbappe's only going to get better after joining Neymar and Edinson Cavani at PSG!

STAT ATTACK!

REST OF EUROPE GOAL MACHINES

9

Lethal hitman Zlatan Ibrahimovic scored in nine games in a row during PSG's 2015-16 title-winning season – a joint-record!

16

Ex-Man. City striker Enes Unal is the youngest scorer in Turkish football history! He was 16 years and 107 days old when he bagged for Bursaspor against Galatasaray in August 2013!

36

No player has scored more goals in a single Serie A season than Gonzalo Higuain – he ripped net 36 times in 2015-16 for Napoli!

71

Roma legend Francesco Totti holds the record for most penalties scored in Serie A history!

35

Luis Suarez scored 35 goals for Ajax in 2009-10 – no foreign player has ever netted more in a single Eredivisie season!

5

Max Kruse is the only player to score for five different Bundesliga teams – St. Pauli, Freiburg, Monchengladbach, Wolfsburg and Werder Bremen!

31
Pierre-Emerick Aubameyang's 31 goals for Dortmund in 2016-17 was the highest number of net-busters by a foreign player in a single Bundesliga season. Legend!
22
When Mauro Icardi jointly won Serie A's top scorer award in 2014-15 aged 22, he became the youngest winner since 1978!
7
Andre Abegglen and Jean Nicolas hold the joint-record for most goals in a single Ligue 1 game – they both hit seven in the 1930s!
5
Celtic legend Henrik Larsson bagged five Scottish Premiership Golden Boots in six seasons between 1998 and 2004 – no player has won more!
4
Robert Lewandowski holds the record for the quickest Bundesliga hat-trick – it took him just four minutes to bag a treble for Bayern against Wolfsburg in September 2015!

Aritz Aduriz

33

Club: ***Athletic Bilbao***

Country: ***Spain*** **DOB:** ***11/2/81***

Bilbao's legendary veteran goal grabber has been proving his doubters wrong for years now! After being written off, Aduriz's peak years have come in his 30s, and the Basque striker could bag over 200 goals for his boyhood club before his career ends!

Andre-Pierre Gignac

32

Club: ***Tigres UANL***

Country: ***France*** **DOB:** ***5/12/85***

Gignac turned down interest from a host of European clubs to sign for Tigres in 2015, and has torn up Mexican footy ever since! The striker scored 28 goals in his first year to win a place in France's Euro 2016 squad, and smashed another 25 last season!

Dries Mertens

31

Club: ***Napoli*** **DOB:** ***6/5/87***

Country: ***Belgium***

As the top goalscorer at Serie A's highest-scoring club last season, Mertens had an unbelievable campaign in 2016-17! He was moved up front because of an injury crisis, but it proved to be a masterstroke as the speedster rammed home 28 league goals!

Alvaro Morata

30

Club: *Chelsea* **DOB:** *23/10/92*

Country: *Spain*

Morata spent most of 2016-17 on Real Madrid's bench, but still ended the season as the club's second top goalscorer in La Liga, getting a goal every 90 minutes on average! He backs up deadly finishing with ace movement, and could become a Chelsea legend!

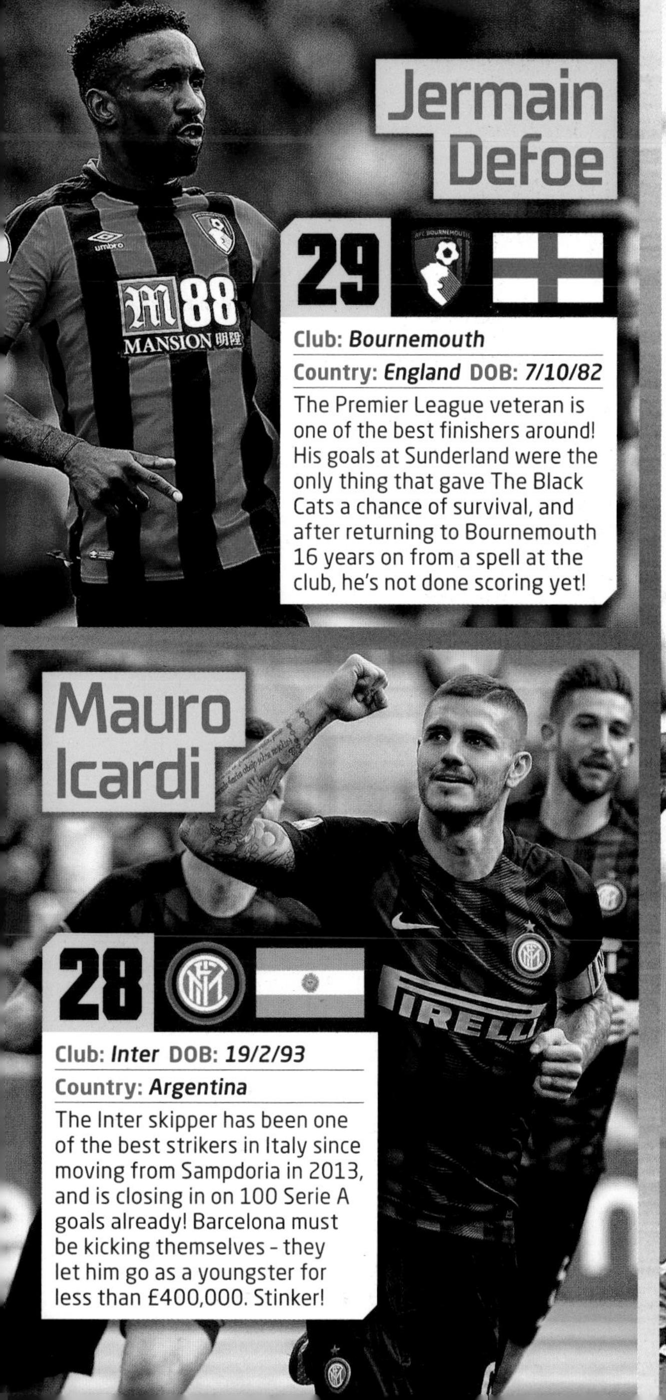

Jermain Defoe

29

Club: *Bournemouth*

Country: *England* **DOB:** *7/10/82*

The Premier League veteran is one of the best finishers around! His goals at Sunderland were the only thing that gave The Black Cats a chance of survival, and after returning to Bournemouth 16 years on from a spell at the club, he's not done scoring yet!

Mauro Icardi

28

Club: *Inter* **DOB:** *19/2/93*

Country: *Argentina*

The Inter skipper has been one of the best strikers in Italy since moving from Sampdoria in 2013, and is closing in on 100 Serie A goals already! Barcelona must be kicking themselves – they let him go as a youngster for less than £400,000. Stinker!

Dele Alli

27

Club: *Tottenham* **DOB:** *11/4/96*

Country: *England*

Alli broke through at MK Dons as an energetic midfielder to seal his move to Tottenham, but he's become an out-and-out No.10 for Spurs. His link-up play, runs into the box and expert finishing have made him one of the most dangerous players in Europe!

Andrea Belotti

26

Club: *Torino* **DOB:** *20/12/93*

Country: *Italy*

Torino's president is such a big fan of Belotti, he slapped a huge £100 million asking price on his striker! With 26 Serie A goals in 2016-17, plenty of big clubs have taken an interest in the sharp shooter, but they'll have to break the bank to get him!

Bas Dost

25

Club: *Sporting* **DOB:** *31/5/89*

Country: *Holland*

After impressing in Holland and Germany with Heerenveen and Wolfsburg, Dost had his best season ever with Sporting in 2016-17! The penalty-box hero smashed 34 league goals in 30 starts, finishing second to Lionel Messi in the Golden Shoe race!

Radamel Falcao

24

Club: *Monaco* **DOB:** *10/2/86*

Country: *Colombia*

Back in 2011-12, Falcao was the best No.9 in the world, hitting 36 goals on the way to winning the Europa League with Atletico! It looked like injuries had ruined his career, but he was back to his best in 2016-17, and inspired Monaco to the Ligue 1 title!

Gareth Bale

23

Club: ***Real Madrid*** **DOB:** ***16/7/89***

Country: ***Wales***

Bale's bagged some huge goals for Real! His first Spanish trophy came after a class strike against Barcelona in the 2014 Copa del Rey Final, and he followed that up by scoring in the CL final too! After an injury-hit 2016-17, this season is a massive one for Gaz!

Javier Hernandez

22

Club: ***West Ham*** **DOB:** ***1/6/88***

Country: ***Mexico***

In five seasons at Man. United, Hernandez scored 37 Prem goals - despite only starting 49 games for The Red Devils! Chicharito loves sniffing out chances in the penalty box, and his movement and poaching instincts have also made him Mexico's record scorer!

Edin Dzeko

21

Club: ***Roma*** **DOB:** ***17/3/86***

Country: ***Bosnia-Herzegovina***

Roma's ace hitman was on fire in 2016-17 as the Serie A giants qualified for the Champo League again! Dzeko finished as the top scorer in Italy with 29 awesome net-busters, and his 50+ goals for Bosnia-Herz. also makes him his country's all-time top scorer!

Jonas

20

Club: *Benfica* **DOB:** *1/4/84*

Country: *Brazil*

We can't believe Jonas has only ever played 12 times for Brazil – he's an absolute goal machine! The clinical finisher's grabbed over 130 goals in all comps in his last seven seasons, and helped Benfica to three league titles in a row. So underrated!

Paulo Dybala

19

Club: *Juventus* **DOB:** *15/11/93*

Country: *Argentina*

Juve were on fire in 2017, and the Argentina young gun played a massive part in that! Dybala doesn't rip net every week, but what he does bring is dynamic dribbling skills and great link-up play with Gonzalo Higuain. He's only going to get better, too!

Alexandre Lacazette

18

Club: *Arsenal* **DOB:** *28/5/91*

Country: *France*

Lacazette's Hypervenom boots have been punishing goalkeepers for ages now! The lightning-fast striker bagged a mind-blowing 28 Ligue 1 goals in just 28 starts for Lyon last campaign, which led to Arsenal stumping up a club record £46.5 million for him!

Thomas Muller

17

Club: *Bayern Munich*

Country: *Germany* **DOB:** *13/9/89*

Muller only scored five league goals last season, but his tallies from previous years mean he has to make it into our Top 20! We reckon he'll be back to his best in 2017-18, particularly as it's a World Cup year – he loves scoring goals at major tournaments!

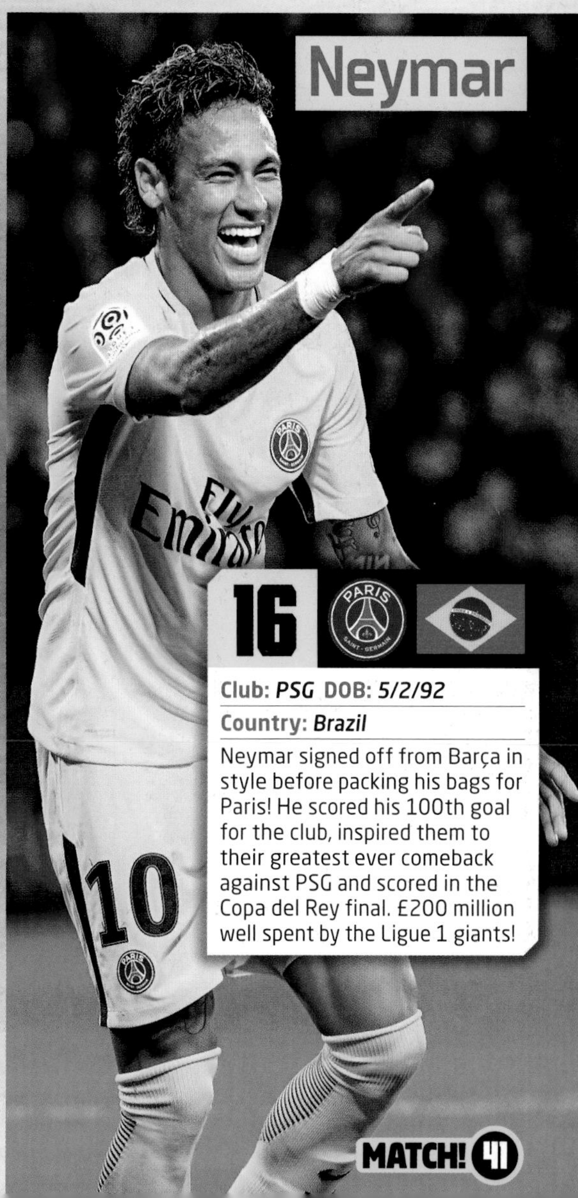

Neymar

16

Club: *PSG* **DOB:** *5/2/92*

Country: *Brazil*

Neymar signed off from Barça in style before packing his bags for Paris! He scored his 100th goal for the club, inspired them to their greatest ever comeback against PSG and scored in the Copa del Rey final. £200 million well spent by the Ligue 1 giants!

STAT ATTACK!

REST OF THE WORLD GOAL MACHINES

21

Kosovo striker Besart Berisha was the top scorer in the A-League last season – he netted every 119 minutes for his club side Melbourne Victory!

13

The top scorer in the 2016-17 South African Premier Soccer League was Cape Town City's Lebogang Manyama – the midfielder scored 13 goals!

145

Former Everton hitman Landon Donovan is the MLS' top scorer ever! The retired striker hit 145 goals between 2001 and 2014!

2

Ice-cool Brazilian Elkeson is the only foreign player to win the Chinese Super League top goalscorer award twice!

5

Football legend Diego Maradona was the Argentine Primera Division's Golden Boot winner five times – that's a joint-record!

7

The fastest goal in MLS history was scored by New York Red Bulls winger Mike Grella! He netted after just seven seconds against Philadelphia Union in 2015!

27

Bradley Wright-Phillips scored 27 goals during the 2014 MLS season – no player's ever hit more in a single campaign!

50

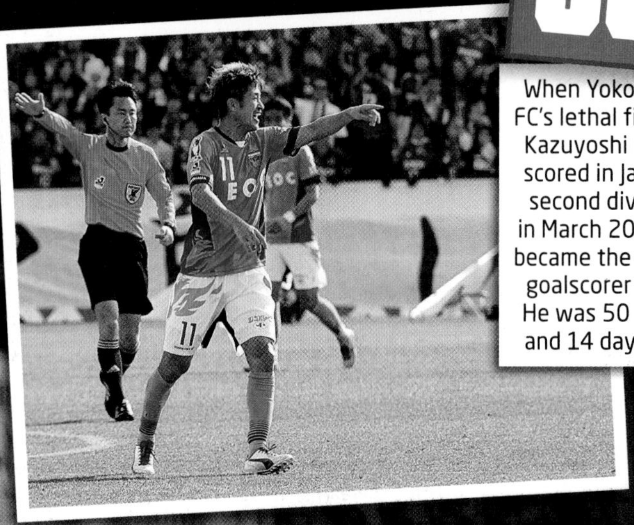

When Yokohama FC's lethal finisher Kazuyoshi Miura scored in Japan's second division in March 2017, he became the oldest goalscorer ever! He was 50 years and 14 days old!

1,283

During his 21-year career, Pele scored a mind-blowing 1,283 goals! You guessed it, that's a world record!

16

Ex-Man. City striker Jo is the youngest scorer in Brazilian Serie A history – he was 16 years and 157 days old when he first bagged for Corinthians in 2003!

131

Ex-Brazil stopper Rogerio Ceni holds the world record for most career goals by a goalkeeper – 131 in total!

Romelu Lukaku

15

Club: *Man. United* DOB: *13/5/93*

Country: *Belgium*

Lukaku's ripped Prem defences to shreds for ages now - he hit 85 goals in his first 186 Premier League games for Chelsea, West Brom and Everton - so it was no surprise when The Red Devils splashed out £75 million on him last summer! He's a total beast!

Alexis Sanchez

14

Club: *Arsenal* DOB: *19/12/88*

Country: *Chile*

Whether Sanch is playing on the wing or as a striker, he's such a dangerous player! The Chile star loves to drive into the penalty area and blast holes in the net with his rocket shots - it's made him the Prem's third-highest scoring South American ever!

Karim Benzema

13

Club: *Real Madrid*

Country: *France* DOB: *19/12/87*

Karim is a real all-round striker - he has great strength, top feet, clinical finishing skills and an epic footy brain! He might not rip net as much as deadly team-mate Cristiano Ronaldo, but he was just as important as Real won La Liga and the CL in 2016-17!

Zlatan Ibrahimovic

12

Club: *Man. United* **DOB:** *3/10/81*

Country: *Sweden*

Zlat looked like he'd been a Prem player for years last season! The big Swede proved he could cut it at any level, bagging 28 goals in all comps for Man. United! After recovering from a knee injury, The Red Devils re-signed him on a one-year deal last summer!

Edinson Cavani

11

Club: *PSG* **DOB:** *14/2/87*

Country: *Uruguay*

Cavani was forever in Zlatan's shadow in Paris, but after a sick season, the Uruguay striker has finished ahead of him in our Top 100 list! His class movement and top shooting skills saw him hit 49 goals in 50 games in all comps - that return is frightening!

Diego Costa

10

Club: *Chelsea* **DOB:** *7/10/88*

Country: *Spain*

Love him or hate him, there's no stopping Diego when he's on the attack! Chelsea's top scorer in their title-winning campaign netted 20 Prem goals, leading The Blues' frontline like a boss! How do you defend against a player with so much power?

Sergio Aguero

9

Club: *Man. City* **DOB:** *2/6/88*

Country: *Argentina*

The City and Argentina legend used his deadly accuracy and ace acceleration to rip defences apart again last season! Despite Gabriel Jesus battling to be the club's No.1 striker, Sergio still scored 33 goals in all comps, including eight in the CL!

Antoine Griezmann

8

Club: *Atletico Madrid*

Country: *France* **DOB:** *21/3/91*

Antoine must have felt sick in 2016 as he finished runner-up in two major finals! He put that disappointment behind him in 2016-17, though – 26 goals in all comps is a quality return! No wonder Europe's top sides are battling it out for his signature!

Harry Kane

7

Club: *Tottenham* **DOB:** *28/7/93*

Country: *England*

2017-18 is a massive season for Kane for both club and country! He'll be hoping to fire Spurs to at least one major trophy, as well as the Golden Boot for himself, plus he'll be key if England want to go far at the 2018 World Cup! What are you made of, Hazza?

Pierre-Emerick Aubameyang

6

Club: *Dortmund* **DOB:** *18/6/89*

Country: *Gabon*

The Bundesliga top scorer was awesome in 2016-17! Defences crumbled at the sight of the mega-quick striker bearing down on goal, as he scored 31 league goals in total! Not only that, but PEA hit the winner as Dortmund won the DFB-Pokal. Legend!

WORDSEARCH

Find last season's Euro Golden Shoe contenders in this grid!

T K O H Z A Q M
R D F T B K X W
H L Z U V B I E
D O G X N Y Q R
N S M X Z U C N
B H Y T Q C W E
B G C Q I E H W M F P M E R H N G O V N B Q R S X L Z D P R
O H T A A I B P U Y T I U M D B D O X D E R B Y S H I R E V
Y J D D V I Q C B F U M A E A C P Y X C M X I B R Q J X M S
C B Z F P A T P C W A Q E V X C R U C P C U T J F M F N E Z
E G U S L C N A Y Z N U Q S H E V U K M A M M E E Q M R H Y
M E R T E N S I B I T I B O S S A L Q I C A R D I B A E M I
Q B Y P M E T W V B L V H A Q I V V I K A F P M R O A M V Y
C K E V S Q O A T L H W C E M M Y D F C I G W X S L R D C F
A L L R Y X D V A E C S T I G E A Y B I T U Y Y Z E D F X Q
I Q W U W N J J Y V Q S R P E R Y I Y X U T F H C W J P P B
M R P C L W N M X E E G A K K G P A F H X Y J P N A U T E V
M I F N J B L T G D H B Q A L X I V N O P S G D F N R N X Q
O E S Q C A V X O E I E M G M I V Z J G S Z S B Y D D L H M
B T X O K B U M B S M L Y U J P Z B D J J W A T L O J V O V
I Z A E O V L P P F O O X E C J V T O W I Z B H W W E B H Q
L X E T D G J J G K K T A R S T E F N M X T V D L S V R Q G
E V I L L O F R Y S V T O O Y B O B D Y C X R O M K I C L C
P T H U Y Z E Z T Z B I A Q M K J C E Q F Q E S T I C C U B
L Q S F X B E V I S L M D Q L U G U Y X X P N T P F Y Y K N
Z I C W O S W A E S J W R D G T N F H D V N R G S H Z U A R
P A X M Z S E I E Y G Y Q L D W T G C E I J C D U E V L K E
B E U W X N J E V G R T N Y E W U L F F Z F V N N D F W U T
Y H E K G X X J J E T V N C B V A Z N C S S A A G E R V Z P
W V D I Y D M E O W K I N J O Y W I A G I U K J L Z X Z H T
Y H S M V H T D E A A H T D W S S O O W Y A Z T V U E E B U
I N P V N Z R T X U S B B I B H T D P W G R E E P H R M A X
I B X K R Z T A G X S P F L E Z L A N F E E B R C C V A A M
W Q O L C E P I U I R W A Z X A O C G T P Z R N N U P S L D
G G Z D Z E H Y Y D Q N D S N P R M R E R M A R V A G N Q O
E B T A M P I X Z F B X W O L Q P X M Y Q S F Y G C F V L C
R V C Q I B G O D Z C D R A X M D O V K P Q I T Z T A K B R
L A U Y X X A L D Y S T M X L N A I B R A H I M O V I C F W
L G B A L E M S W X L A O J J B I R V U J M Q B X T U U K N
H J C U D C U H Z A I R I D U W Z V H D Z E K O O R L Y R X

Aguero	Boyce	Dzeko	Kane	Modeste
Alli	Cavani	Higuain	Lacazette	Ronaldo
Aspas	Costa	Ibrahimovic	Lewandowski	Sanchez
Aubameyang	Derbyshire	Icardi	Lukaku	Soares
Belotti	Djurdjevic	Immobile	Mertens	Suarez
Berg	Dost	Insigne	Messi	Werner

FOOTY MIS-MATCH

Study these two pics carefully, then see if you can find the ten differences between them!

ANSWERS ON PAGE 60

Gonzalo
Higuain
BOOTS
NIKE HYPERVENOM
5
Club: Juventus DOB: 10/12/87
Country: Argentina
Nobody's scored more Serie A goals than Gonzo since he moved to Italy in 2013! His tally of 36 in 2015-16 matched the all-time record for goals in a season too, and that convinced Juventus to make him the most expensive player in the league's history!

Robert Lewandowski

Club: *Bayern Munich*

Country: *Poland* **DOB:** *21/8/88*

Lewa has been an unstoppable net-busting machine in Germany for years, first for Dortmund and now with Bayern! He's won the Bundesliga's Golden Boot award twice, and in 2015 hit nine goals in just five minutes. He goes to sleep dreaming about goals!

DID YOU KNOW?

The Poland skipper has scored 25 goals or more in all comps in each of the last six seasons!

Luis Suarez

BOOTS

ADIDAS X 17+

3

Club: *Barcelona* **DOB:** *24/1/87*

Country: *Uruguay*

In 2013-14, Suarez matched the Prem record for most goals in a 38-game season, and since moving to Spain he's carried on that form! In 2015-16, the Barça goal machine beat Lionel Messi and Cristiano Ronaldo to the top scorer award – he's that clinical!

DID YOU KNOW?

It took Uruguay's all-time top goalscorer just 120 games to bust 100 nets for Barça!

Lionel Messi

2

Club: *Barcelona* **DOB:** *24/6/87*

Country: *Argentina*

As the all-time top goalscorer for Barcelona, Argentina and La Liga, Leo is the definition of a lethal finisher! After netting 91 times in 2012, he broke the record for most goals in a calendar year, and he's bagged over 40 in each of the last eight seasons. Ledge!

DID YOU KNOW?

Lethal Leo has won the European Golden Shoe award a joint-record four times!

Cristiano Ronaldo

Club: ***Real Madrid*** **DOB:** ***5/2/85***

Country: ***Portugal***

2017 was Ronaldo's year! The Real Madrid legend once again finished as the club's top scorer with 25 league goals to finally reclaim the Spanish title, and he was even better in the Champo League! With ten goals in the knockout stages, including two in the CL final, CR7 delivered when it mattered most, proving why he's the planet's No.1 goal machine. Bravo, Cristiano!

DID YOU KNOW?

Ronaldo has been the Champions League's top scorer in each of the last five seasons!

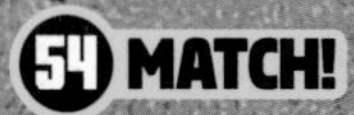

BOOTS
NIKE MERCURIAL

TOP 100... STAT ATTACK!

You've seen our Top 100 Goal Machines countdown, now check out the lethal finishers by club, country, age and more!

600

Only one player in our Top 100 has scored 600 goals in their career - Cristiano Ronaldo!

TOP 100 BY... 2016-17 GOALS!

PLAYER/CLUB	GOALS
Lionel Messi *Barcelona*	37
Edinson Cavani *PSG*	35
Bas Dost *Sporting*	34
Pierre-Emerick Aubameyang *Dortmund*	31
Robert Lewandowski *Bayern Munich*	30
Edin Dzeko *Roma*	29
Harry Kane *Tottenham*	29
Luis Suarez *Barcelona*	29
Alexandre Lacazette *Lyon*	28
Dries Mertens *Napoli*	28

TOP 100 BY... CLUB!

CLUB	NO. OF PLAYERS
Chelsea	5
Liverpool	4
Man. United	4
Tottenham	4
Arsenal	3
Atletico Madrid	3
Bayern Munich	3
Everton	3
Juventus	3
Napoli	3
PSG	3
Real Madrid	3
AC Milan	2
Ajax	2
Barcelona	2
Bournemouth	2
Celtic	2
Leicester	2
Man. City	2
Newcastle	2
Sporting	2
Villarreal	2
Watford	2
Other	37

10

The lethal finisher with the most World Cup goals from our quality list is Thomas Muller - he's got ten!

TOP 100 BY... BOOTS!

BOOTS	NO. OF PLAYERS
Nike Mercurial	27
adidas X	25
Nike Hypervenom	20
adidas ACE	7
Puma ONE	7
adidas Nemeziz	5
Nike Tiempo	3
Nike Magista	2
Puma evoPOWER	2
Puma evoSPEED	1
New Balance Furon	1

TOP 100 BY... LEAGUE!

LEAGUE	NO. OF PLAYERS
Premier League	39
La Liga	12
Serie A	12
Ligue 1	7
Bundesliga	6
Eredivisie	4
MLS	4
Primeira Liga	4
Chinese Super League	3
Super Lig	3
Scottish Premiership	2
A-League	1
Indian Super League	1
Liga MX	1
USL Second Division	1

TOP 100 BY... AGE!

TOP 10 YOUNGEST

PLAYER	AGE
Kylian Mbappe	18
Marcus Rashford	19
Kasper Dolberg	19
Tammy Abraham	19
Gabriel Jesus	20
Moussa Dembele	21
Dele Alli	21
Timo Werner	21
Anthony Martial	21
Andre Silva	21

TOP 10 OLDEST

PLAYER	AGE
Didier Drogba	39
Tim Cahill	37
Robbie Keane	37
Peter Crouch	36
Aritz Aduriz	36
Samuel Eto'o	36
Ruben Castro	36
Zlatan Ibrahimovic	35
David Villa	35
Jermain Defoe	34

All ages correct up to the start of the 2017-18 season.

146

The player with the most international caps in our Top 100 list is Republic Of Ireland legend Robbie Keane!

Golden oldie Samuel Eto'o made his pro debut back in 1997 - no player in our list debuted any earlier than that!

1997

TOP 100 BY... COUNTRY!

COUNTRY	NO. OF PLAYERS
England	13
France	11
Spain	10
Argentina	6
Brazil	6
Italy	6
Belgium	5
Holland	5
Germany	3
Colombia	2
Croatia	2
Denmark	2
Ivory Coast	2
Poland	2
Portugal	2
Uruguay	2

4

No player in our list has won more Champions League trophies at one club than Lionel Messi!

DRAW YOUR FAVE GOAL MACHINE!

You've seen our countdown of the Top 100 Goal Machines – now why not sketch your fave star for the chance to win an ace prize?

WIN!

Just photocopy this page, draw your fave player and send your drawing to:
Goal Machines 2018
MATCH Magazine
Kelsey Media
14 Priestgate
Peterborough
Cambs PE1 1JA

Then we'll pick our fave picture and send the winner a pair of Nike Hypervenom boots, thanks to Lovell Soccer!

CLOSING DATE:
January 31, 2018.

Name:

Date of birth:

Address:

Boot size:

Mobile:

Email:

Face In The Crowd P29

Brain-Buster P28

1. 2011
2. False
3. No.10
4. Man. United
5. Nike
6. Colombia
7. Barcelona
8. Diego Costa
9. Left
10. Borussia Dortmund

Wordsearch P48

```
T K O H                                               Z A Q M
R D F T                                               B K X W
H L Z U                                               V B I E
D O G X                                               N Y Q R
N S M X                                               Z U C N
B H Y T                                               Q C W E
B G C Q I E H W M F P M E R H N G O V N B Q R S X L Z O P R
O H T A A I B P U Y T I U M D B D O X D E R B Y S H I R E V
Y J D D V I Q C B F U M A E A C P Y X C M X I B R Q J X M S
C B Z F P A T P C W A Q E V X C R U C P C U T J F M F N E Z
E G U S L C N A Y Z N U Q S H E V U K M A M M E E Q M R H Y
M E R T E N S I B I T I B O S S A L Q I C A R D I B A E M I
Q B Y P M E T W V B L V H A Q I V V I K A F P M R O A M V Y
C K E V S Q O A T L H W C E M M Y D F C I G W X S L R D C F
A L L R Y X D V A E C S T I G E A Y B I T U Y Y Z E D F X Q
I Q W U W N J J Y V Q S R P E R Y I Y X U T F H C W J P P B
M R P C L W N M X E E G A K K G P A F H X Y J P N A U T E V
M I F N J B L T G D H B Q A L X I V N O P S G D F N R N X Q
O E S Q C A V X O E I E M G M I V Z J G S Z S B Y O D L H M
B T X O K B U M B S M L Y U J P Z B D J J W A T L O J V O V
I Z A E O V L P P F O O X E C J V T O W I Z B H W W E B H Q
L X E T O G J J G K K T A R S T E F N M X T V D L S V R Q G
E V I L L O F R Y S V T O O Y B O B D Y C X R O M K I C L C
P T H U Y Z E Z T Z B I A Q M K J C E Q F Q E S T I C C U B
L Q S F X B E V I S L M D Q L U G U Y X X P N T P F Y Y K N
Z I C W O S W A E S J W R D G T N F H D V N R G S H Z U A R
P A X M Z S E I E Y G Y Q L D W T G C E I J C D U E V L K E
B E U W X N J E V G R T N Y E W U L F F Z F V N N D F W U T
Y H E K G X X J J E T V N C B V A Z N C S S A A G E R V Z P
W V D I Y D M E O W K I N J D Y W I A G I U K J L Z X Z H T
Y H S M V H T D E A A H T D W S S O O W Y A Z T V U E E B U
I N P V N Z R T X U S B B I B H T D P W G R E E P H R M A X
I B X K R Z T A G X S P F L E Z L A N F E E B R C C V A A M
W Q O L C E P I U I R W A Z X A O C G T P Z R N N U P S L D
G G Z D Z E H Y Y D Q N D S N P R M R E R M A R V A G N Q O
E B T A M P I X Z F B X W O L Q P X M Y Q S F Y G C F V L C
R V C Q I B G O D Z C D R A X M D O V K P Q I T Z T A K B R
L A U Y X X A L D Y S T M X L N A I B R A H I M O V I C F W
L G B A L E M S W X L A O J J B I R V U J M Q B X T U U K N
H J C U D C U H Z A I R I D U W Z V H D Z E K O O R L Y R X
```

Footy Mis-Match P49